PROLOGUE

I grew up in a rooming house at the Jersey Shore in Point Pleasant Beach. My family and I lived with strangers and some longtime guests who were mostly drunks and drug addicts. It was the perfect setting for some incredible stories, which I'll share with you.

I was divorced many years ago and have gone on dozens of blind dates. Most of them were doozies! I'll tell you all about them.

I've had more "What are the Odds of That?" kinds of stories than most people. I think you'll find them pretty amazing.

In my writing, you'll see that I struggled to provide clear segues as I moved from one story to the next. I have a few flavors of stories; the only common denominator is me. Sorry about that. They're my stories. Mostly funny, some sad, but all true. I promise you will laugh.

STOP ME IF I TOLD YOU THIS ONE

Eileen Flarity Laterza

CHAPTER ONE – LOSERS' JUNCTION

CHAPTER TWO – OUT INTO THE REAL WORLD

CHAPTER THREE – BLIND DATES GONE WRONG

CHAPTER FOUR – WHAT ARE THE ODDS OF THAT?

CHAPTER FIVE – MORE PRETTY GOOD STORIES

CHAPTER ONE – LOSERS' JUNCTION

Big, thick coke-bottle glasses. A polyester, flower print dress with a matching belt around the waist. Stockings, the kind you can't see through, pilly, and chunky. Black, sensible shoes. Soft, grey hair, held in place with a dozen brown bobby pins. Aunt Bea Rafferty. She'd emigrated from Ireland as a young lady, but still had a strong Irish brogue. Like her fellow countrymen, she was destined to be a drunk or a teetotaler. For many Irish, there's nothing in between. Aunt Bea loved her tea.

July 1969. A dreary, rainy weekend at the Jersey Shore. We all gathered in the living room of the Mount Vernon Guest House. The U.S. had just landed a spaceship on the moon. As the rain poured down outside, we awaited the moment when the astronauts would immerge from the capsule. "That's what's causing the rain, you know," Winnie pronounced. In her early thirties, and from Ireland as well, she was certain that the unnatural journey to the moon had caused a disturbance in the world's meteorology. "We're not supposed to be there, and God is paying us back. If God wanted us on the moon, he'd have strapped rockets to our arses."

The moment had arrived. We'd waited well over an hour. As Neil Armstrong began his now famous euphemism "One small step for Man…" there was a clinking of teacups. Aunt Bea emerged from the kitchen with a tray of cups, and a steaming pot of water. "…One giant…" "Would anyone care for some tea?" she asked as she stepped in front of the television. "…leap for Mankind." There she stood. A sweet smile on her face, the tray extended, hands shaking with age, smack in front of the TV.

"Sweet Mary, Mother of God, Bea, we missed the whole damn thing!" screeched Winnie.

Winnie Brennan Flarity and Paul Flarity. My Mom and Dad. Proprietors of The Mount Vernon Guest House, Point Pleasant Beach, NJ. One block from the ocean and boardwalk. It was later named "Losers' Junction" by one of the guests who had a sign made for us to replace the Mt. Vernon sign on the front lawn. Rooms available daily $6, Weekly $35. Swimming pool, outdoor grill, clean sheets weekly, coffee and donuts in the foyer Saturdays and Sundays only. No meals served, no kitchen privileges. For young ladies, no gentlemen allowed in rooms.

Every Friday it was sheet-changing day. I dreaded it. Since moving to Losers' Junction at age 10, and being the oldest of the three kids, I was assigned to sheet changing duty. I grabbed as many sheets as I could carry to save trips from the laundry room to the 2nd and 3rd floors. They were all flat sheets. No fitted sheets. So, I could stack quite a few. I'd stack them so high that they covered my face, but I knew how many steps I had to climb. I'd count to 21 and know I'd be at the 2nd floor landing. To my left was the door leading to room 9 on the 3rd floor, also known as the "penthouse." Nothing luxurious about it. Just an open room with four single beds and one double bed. The young, single guys from North Jersey would stay up there on weekends.

Next was room 4, with 2 double beds. That was home to the Bird Man for many years. He kept several canaries in his room, which would scare the bejesus out of me when he'd let them loose. I think that fear was rooted in my time spent on my adoptive grandparents' farm. They were distant cousins of my grandfather, the Curtins. When my Mom came from Ireland, they took her in. When we would later visit as small kids, my grandfather insisted that we eat all our oatmeal. My sister and brother liked it, but I hated it. To ensure that I ate all my oatmeal, he would put his pet canary on my head and had it stay there until all my oatmeal was gone. I've been afraid of birds ever since.

Room 5 was at the end of the hall. It was a long, narrow room with windows on 3 sides. Bernard lived there for many years. He was a talented artist and a complete drunk. Raised in Germany, he lived through the bombings of Berlin in World War II. Every night he'd have awful nightmares and scream out in his sleep. As a kid, I called him "Barnyard." Not so funny, but at 12 years old, I thought it was. Barnyard had a long beard. He would often pass out while sitting in the rocking chair in our living room after too many vodkas. One night when I suppose I'd had enough of Barnyard's drunkenness, and I shaved off *half* his beard.

Room 6, with one double bed, was my room for many winters. We weren't allowed to have a room of our own in the summers. They were for the guests. But every winter we made one room our own. The decision wasn't too tough. They were all equally outdated and all had mattresses with broken springs that would dig into your ass if you turned too quickly. For holiday weekends in the summer, we'd sleep in the garage on pool lounge chairs, the kind with woven, rough plastic. We'd wake up with the imprint of the chairs on our cheeks…both face and ass.

Room 7 was the largest room with two double beds and a closet that was shared with room 6. For many summers a young woman named Gail Story and her friends would stay in Room 7. My father called them Gail Story and her 4 chapters.

Room 8 had a double bed and a linoleum floor. Well, I guess all the rooms had a linoleum floor. Stasha Matesky from Russia lived there. He was about twenty years old with a strong Russian accent and a giant unibrow. I don't what it was about Stasha, but as kids we loved to tease him.

We'd knock on his bedroom door and run away and hide. Giggling when we heard him answer the door asking, "who's there?" We'd do it again 10 minutes later and he'd fall for it again.

After Stasha moved out, room 8 was my room for a few winters. I remember my little white, vinyl record player I kept on my dresser in front of my mirror. It played 45's. I would stand in front of my mirror and sing into my hairbrush the hits of the day. My little white record player only lasted a couple of years. One teenage night, after drinking with my friends, I got up in the middle of the night, felt sick, and lifted the lid of my little, white record player which I must have mistaken for a toilet, vomited, closed the lid and went back to bed.

I was sleeping in Room 8 where my little Jack Russel terrier was sleeping on my robe on the floor across the room. Kerri didn't care for any people besides our family. She was mischievous and adorable. She would often leave the house, and cross two streets to the lake. She knew when to wait for cars to pass by and always made it home safely. Her mission at the lake was to roll in the goose poop. So back to Room 8, I awoke in the middle of the night and heard squeaking. The light switch was at the other end of the room, so I couldn't see where the squeaking was coming from. Assuming it was a mouse, I started throwing items from my nightstand towards the sound of the squeaks. First a Chapstick, then a hairbrush, then paperbacks. But the squeaking continued. I didn't want to step on the mouse so I stood up on the bed and walked to the foot and took a giant leap toward the light switch so my feet would only touch the floor twice. I turned on the light and saw Kerry on my robe with four little puppies and all the things from my nightstand surrounding her. We didn't even know she was pregnant.

My middle school friend and I were always looking for adventures. With our hometown being surrounded by water on three sides, by the river, the ocean, and the inlet, we found lots of dangerous things to do. One of our favorites was to pack a lunch and crawl down into the jetty rocks at the inlet. The jetty was a long series of giant rocks placed between the inlet, connecting the ocean, the river, and the beach. There were caverns in the jetty rocks which we could crawl into and set up a little picnic. There was one factor that never seemed to occur to us, and that was the rising tide. There were lots of close calls, scurrying out of the jetty just before the ocean water would have filled our little picnic cavern.

Later, in high school, that same middle school friend and I were still getting ourselves in rough spots. One night we were out at a bar in Belmar, NJ and took a liking to two young brothers. After a night of drinking, they invited us back to their house where they lived with their parents. We had to be very quiet, sneaking up the stairs to their bedroom. They had two single beds, so my friend and I pared off with the brothers, making out like teens do. Suddenly we heard their Mom coming up the stairs yelling, "I know you have someone up here!" We all panicked. My friend hid in the closet, and I went behind the shower curtain in the bathroom. The guys just acted like Mom was crazy and convinced her no one was there. After she went back downstairs, the guys said we had to leave. "I'm not going down those stairs!" my friend and I both said. So, the guys opened their bedroom window and all four of us crawled out onto the roof and down the side of the house. It was now about 4am and we had no ride home to Point Pleasant Beach, which was about 8 miles away. My friend and I started walking home. Once we got to a major street, we started hitchhiking. It took about a half hour for someone to pick us up. It was a pickup truck filled with bales of hay. The gentleman said "Sure, I can give you a ride, just hop up on there!" So, we climbed atop the bales. It was a long ride home because the hay guy had to make a couple of stops to drop off hay. The sun was just coming up as my friend and I made our way down the main street in our town, thanked the hay man, and walked the rest of the way to our homes.

As in most high schools, gym teachers would choose two students to pick basketball teams. I was a decent athlete, so I was typically one of the captains. The way it's supposed to work is the captains would start with picking the best players and work their way down to those who weren't so good. My dear friend wasn't so good. So, when it was announced that teams would be picked, she'd try to sneak out of the gym, knowing no one would want her on their team anyway. But not when I was captain. I would announce "I'm picking the best player I know!" And I'd point to my friend.

At 15, I worked at a fast food, seafood restaurant called the Kettle of Fish in Point Pleasant Beach. It was so much fun because I worked with several of my friends as well as my sister and brother. Stephen was always getting in trouble. He was the pot washer. Whenever I worked a shift that followed his I would inevitably hear someone yelling because Stephen had once again hidden the dirty pots rather than wash them.

The manager was our friend who lived nearby in an apartment. She would often have parties that we were invited to despite our being underage. One very busy Saturday night, a night when our manager was having a party, I went to the back room of the restaurant and turned off all the electrical breakers. There were about 60 people seated at the tables outside, now in the dark. I went out and apologized and asked politely for everyone to leave. Off to the party we went.

I have 35 first cousins, so when we were young, we always had lots of kids to play with. They all have great memories of staying at our house in the summertime, swimming in the pool, going to the boardwalk, and getting into trouble.

My mom loved having all the nieces and nephews stay at the house. She loved seeing us have fun and making sure we had enough to eat. Being Irish, she wasn't the greatest cook. Mostly meat and potatoes and an occasional pea soup. My cousin and I were sitting on the front porch having some stew Mom had made. My cousin took one spoonful and gagged. She then took the bowl and dumped the stew into the bushes. My mom came out to the porch a bit later holding the pot of stew. Seeing that my cousin had finished every bit of it, she filled her bowl again.

Rooms 1, 2 & 3 were on the first floor. Rooms 1 & 2 were very small with only 1 single bed each. Room 3 was my parents' room. My Mom was born in Roscommon, Ireland and had 8 siblings. They lived in a small 3-bedroom thatched roof cottage. The parents had one room, all the kids slept in another, and the cow had the 3rd room. Like so many Irish in those days, they were extremely poor. We have only a few pictures of them from that time, but in this one they all show that they were obviously dressed in their

Sunday best, with winter coats, but most had no shoes.

My Mom had to leave Ireland when she was 14. Her mom had died of TB when the youngest child was 2. Her dad tried to hold it together but realized he couldn't raise the kids properly. He had to ship the younger ones off to strangers in America; relatives he'd never met. The sadness he must have felt sending them off, one by one, knowing he'd likely never see them again. My Mom sailed on a ship, alone, from Ireland to New Jersey. She hadn't gotten much of an education in Ireland and so had to go to school with kids much younger than her. It was a very exciting day for her when she graduated from grammar school. It was a Catholic school, and the ceremony was in the church. She had never known what it was like to have anything fancy. Never had any jewelry or nice clothing. So, when the Curtins gave her a new watch for her graduation, she was over the moon. As she walked up the center aisle of the church, she wore the watch on her right hand so everyone on that side of the church could see it. When she got her diploma and returned going down the outer aisle, she moved the watch to her left hand so everyone on that side of the church could see it.

When she was 16, she reunited with two of her sisters, and they lived together in Newark, NJ. They found themselves spending a lot of time at McGovern's Tavern. The owner, Frank McGovern, also from Ireland, took the girls under his wing. He would whisk them from the bar to the "backroom" where he felt they were safer. The backroom is where all the Irish dances took place. My dad, Paul, was a bartender at McGovern's and took a liking to my Mom. Soon after meeting her, my Dad went into the service. After serving time in the Army, he was then accepted into the U.S. Naval Academy. He would tell me stories about how very difficult it was to be a plebe, then a midshipman at the Academy. His plebe year, or freshman year, 9 classmates jumped from the three-story stairway onto the marble floor below, committing suicide. His first midshipman year he failed physics and didn't return the next year. My parents were married soon after that and started a family in West Orange, NJ.

There was a sweet innocence to my Mom. She was always the brunt of our jokes, and she always shrugged it off saying "Ah, shut your gub! You'll miss me when I'm gone!" in her lyrical Irish brogue. Once in the '70's, Dad was awarded a beautiful clock after twenty-five years of service with the NJ Department of Transportation. She placed it up on the fireplace mantel and pointed out to us that it was a "really good brand. Look, it's a Quartz!" she exclaimed.

My mom was raised Irish Catholic. Prayer was important to her, and she wanted to instill that in us kids. Every night, before bed, she would have my sister, brother and I kneel in front of her, and we'd say our prayers. The "Lord's Prayer" and a "Hail Mary." Then we'd all bless ourselves in Gaelic, "In aham an Athar, agus a Mhic, agus am Spiroraid, Naomh. Amen." I remember how to say it to this day.

When I was a kid, I was a bit of an entrepreneur. I started earning money at age 11 by making potholders and selling them door to door. There was a square, metal loom with teeth on all four sides. I'd take cotton loops, in lots of colors, and attached them to opposite sides of the loom. I'd weave the loops through the other loops until I had a nice, tight square. I'd then tie off the ends and voila, I'd have a potholder. I'd wander through the neighborhood, door to door, selling them for 20 cents each.

My next job was as a newspaper girl. Every week "The Reporter" newspaper would drop off 50 newspapers to my house. I'd sit on a stool, hang the plastic newspaper clear plastic bags on a doorknob, roll up the papers, one by one, and stuff them into the bags. The next morning I'd cram all the papers into large baskets on either side of the back of my bike. I'd ride through the neighborhoods, tossing the papers on my customers' lawns. I earned 5 cents per paper. When my brother got a little older, I helped him get the same job. He didn't last long at it. Rather than rolling up all the papers and stuffing them into the plastics bags and delivering them, he hid them all in the bushes in front of our house.

My Dad was the authoritarian of the house. We all had assigned chores but always seemed to wait until the last minute when he got home to perform them. All three of us, my mom, brother, and sister would lounge in the living room watching TV waiting for Dad to come home. Each of us would be prepared to launch into action. I'd have the pile of clean sheets in my lap, Mom would be holding the handle of the vacuum, my sister would have the Pledge and dust rag in hand, my brother would have nothing in his hand. He was a rebel. The second we heard his car pulling in the stone driveway, we'd leap into action.

Dad had a loud, booming sneeze. If he sneezed in the kitchen, we could hear it all over the house. Many times, I'd have to run down two flights of stairs to say, "God bless you."

My Dad was born in Newark, NJ and grew up in Avon-by-the-Sea. He was a pretty good piano player and would play for the nuns at his parents' house every Sunday. He was taught by Eddie Layton who was the accomplished organ player who performed at Yankee Stadium. When my Dad was 17, Eddie told him "I can't teach you anything more. You have surpassed me in talent." At 18, my Dad played at Carnegie Hall and Radio City Music Hall. Soon after he went into the Service. When he returned, he never played again. Never even touched a keyboard. He felt that he had been forced to play for so many years and no longer loved it.

Despite never playing an instrument again, my Dad loved to sing. Family gatherings were often a place where we would all sing Irish songs and American folk songs. That tradition continues today with the Flarity family.

As kids growing up with the boardwalk and amusement rides just a block from our house, we were lucky to take advantage of all the fun it had to offer. One of the best things about summer was that there were fireworks on the beach every Thursday night. Through the years we would join all locals and Bennies in standing on the boardwalk watching the fireworks and collectively marveling with lots of "oooohs" and "ahhhhhs." Over time we became a little jaded regarding the fireworks and decided to enjoy those Thursday nights in a different way. We would crawl under the boardwalk with a dollar bill. We'd stick it through a crack in the boardwalk, wait to see someone reaching down to grab it, and quickly snatch it away, laughing our heads off.

Me at 12 years old: "I can never be a bus driver." Friend: "Why?" Me: "Because Flarity will get you nowhere."

We had such a mix of people staying at Losers' Junction. Some were families who would come for a week in the summer, some were young people who would come for weekend to enjoy the Shore bars and boardwalk. Others were drunks and drug addicts who would stay year-round. We had very little privacy. The living room was a "common area" shared with the guests. The only private rooms were bedrooms, the kitchen, and a bathroom the family used. Our front door was always unlocked because the guests didn't have keys. The police did not need a search warrant to enter the house because we had a rooming house license, which technically made the property accessible to the public. I remember being awoken a few nights to the sound of police radios outside my bedroom door. There was a drug addict living in the room next to me and the cops arrested him a few times. There were a few long-term guests who seemed like genuinely good people. When I was 14, I worked a summer job on the boardwalk at "Ray's Lucky Spot." It was a wheel where you could win a big wicker basket of household/food products. It was 10 cents a try. I worked there 7 days a week for $1.10/hour. I loved making my own money. One of the long terms guests was Charlie. He was a nice guy with a drinking problem. He was having trouble because he needed to drive to Florida to see his sick mom but didn't have the money for gas/tolls to get down there. It was the end of the summer and I had saved $150. I loaned the money to Charlie who promised me he'd pay me back when he returned to New Jersey. I never saw Charlie again.

When I was 13 my mom and dad went to Ireland and left us in the care of my aunt. Being a bit on the mischievous side, my cousin, who was 14, managed to get a bottle of Boone's Farm wine. Neither of us had ever drank before, so we were nervous. We decided to go down to the woods by the railroad tracks in Manasquan, NJ after it got dark. As we crossed the street towards the tracks, a police car came toward us. My cousin freaked out and threw the bottle into the woods. Of course, the cop saw that and pulled over. He asked what we were doing and though I can't remember exactly what we said, I'm sure it was a big, fat fib. We were taken to the police station where we were patted down. They scared the bejesus out of us; I'm sure that was the intent. They asked for my parents' phone number, and I explained they were in Ireland. They called my aunt who came and picked us up. She said she would not tell my parents, but that I had to promise to tell them. It was no problem to tell my mom. She was easy. The problem was telling my Dad. He could be tough. I got up the courage to go into the kitchen one evening where he was enjoying his nightly Bud beer and Pall Malls. I'm sure I was visibly shaking while I explained to him what happened. Who knows what terrible punishment I might get. I told the story and there was silence. Dad put his head down with his thumb and fingers on his forehead. There was a long, painful pause. Finally, he raised his head slowly and said, "Couldn't you have picked a better wine?"

In our middle school years my friend and I were always looking for mischief. A few times we would sneak onto the NJ Transit train in Point Pleasant Beach and run right into the bathroom without paying the fare. When we heard the stop for Spring Lake, we'd run out of the bathroom and off the train. It was a short walk to Mike Doolan's Hotel where they had a pool for the hotel guests. We'd spend the afternoon pretending to be guests, swimming in the pool, then heading back to the bathroom on the train.

My Mom was a teetotaler until her mid-thirties when we moved into Losers' Junction. She started feeling obligated to entertain the guests in the summer by the pool and started joining in on the drinking. It didn't take long for her to be drinking every day, even into the winter. I remember making it my job to search the house for her vodka bottles. I'd either empty them out or replace the vodka with water. It was a futile effort to get her to stop. By the time I was 14, 4 years after moving into Losers' Junction, she was in rehab. It was tough for us because she was gone over Christmas. But we were so happy when she came home sober. That didn't last for too long. My Mom struggled with depression and addiction for several years later. When I was 19, I returned from college to spend the weekend at home. I got there late on a Friday night and found a note on the kitchen table from my mom. "I've taken all the pills. I'm in Room 4." I raced upstairs to find my mom passed out on the bed. I tried to wake her but couldn't. I pulled her off the bed onto the floor shaking her and yelling for her to please wake up. I called the ambulance and got her to the hospital. They pumped her stomach and revived her. I slept with her in the hospital that night. My fear of this happening again never left me.

My friends had a house on the beach in Point Pleasant Beach. It was often the party house in high school. One night we all decided to stay up all night so we could watch the sunrise. After it rose, I didn't want to go straight home because I knew my Dad would be leaving for work around that time and I didn't want him to see me pulling into the driveway as he was pulling out. So, I needed a Plan B. Next to my friends' house was the Beacon Manor Motel. I decided I would use one of their rooms for a nap and head home later in the morning. I was able to slide a window open and crawl into a motel room. I fell fast asleep only to be awoken a couple of hours later by the clanking of a housekeeper's cart. As she entered the room, I shot up in bed and asked in an accusatory tone "HOW DARE YOU??" as if she'd committed some heinous crime. Thinking she had entered the wrong room, she quickly left, allowing me to skedaddle.

One summer we had five French kids staying at Losers' Junction. We helped get them local jobs and tried to make them feel welcome. They were my age, about 17, so I introduced them to my friends. We learned that one of them was a medium in Paris, which really intrigued us. So, we decided to have a séance. Chantel, the medium, instructed us to carry a big, heavy, round dining room table to a specific bedroom upstairs. She said that was the room where she was feeling a spirit. Seven or eight of us sat around the table, with our hands on the table, touching pinkies. I was very skeptical. I was on the lookout for anything that seemed staged or fake. Chantel began her process, calling on spirits to visit us. After a minute or two, the table began to wobble. We all kept our hands on the table, with pinkies touching. Then the table began to really jump from left to right. It was hard to keep our hands on the table, so we all pushed our seats back with our butts. Suddenly the table shot across the room to the door, knocking down two of my friends. When everything settled down, Chantel explained to us that there was a little 4-year-old girl who had drowned in the ocean behind this beach house. She was supposed to have been taken care of by a nanny, but the nanny wasn't watching closely that day. She gave us the date and year in which it happened. My friend whose parents owned the house went to the library to look at old newspapers on microfiche from 75 years prior and found the story of the little girl who drowned there.

My high school friends and I loved to go camping in the woods during the summer. It really wasn't so much about our love of the outdoors as it was chance for all of us to get together and have some beers around the campfire. During one trip, we spent the night drinking and laughing. There were no toilet facilities, so we had to go into the woods to pee. When it was time to get our tent out of the trunk of the car, it began to rain. My friend who owned the car couldn't find her keys. She guessed that they'd fallen out of her back pocket while on one of her pee outings. The rain started coming down harder. We all searched the surrounding woods for the keys with no luck. The best we could do was spend the night sleeping under the car and wait till daylight to search for the keys. There we were, all five of us sleeping beneath a little Datsun.

The next year we wised up and rented a Lean-To on the campground. It's a little wooden cabin that could sleep all of us. One friend had called ahead to make the reservation. We waited in line at the campground to get the keys to the Lean-To. When it was our turn, our friend told the employee that we reserved the Leanato. The employee had a blank stare, not sure what she was talking about. "Lee-a-NA-tow!" she enunciated loudly. The employee still didn't know what she was talking about. The others waiting in line behind us were getting a little restless and my friend insisted once again that we reserved a "Lee-a-NA-tow."

"Oh!" said the employee, "you mean a Lean-To!"

In my teen years, I was a waitress at Jack Baker's Wharfside Restaurant in Point Pleasant Beach. I made some great friends there. We often went out for drinks after work to Jimmy Byrne's Sea Girt Inn. It was a big, two-story, older building. The bar was on the second floor. The Jerry Lynch band often played there. You could actually feel the floor going up and down when everyone sang and danced. Along the wall, there were cases of beer stacked up. I don't know what came over me, but when we were leaving, I grabbed a case of beer and headed downstairs. Jimmy Byrnes always had a wall of big, burly bouncers standing near the exit. As I sashayed by them with my beer, one of them asked where I was going with the case. I explained that we didn't have a lot of money, so we brought our own case hoping we could drink it here. But they made me leave it downstairs, so I'm just taking it home now. And off I went into the parking lot where my friends were driving away in embarrassment. "Wait for me!" I said while running through the lot carrying the case.

After Jimmy Byrnes last call, we'd go to Dunkin Donuts. It was always very crowded cause it was closing time for the bars. One night, we were standing in line for a while, with maybe 20 people ahead of us. Our friend, Darryl, disappeared and suddenly reappeared behind the counter with the little white, paper hat on his head, towering above the other workers with his 6'4" frame, taking orders from us.

It was my last night working at the Wharfside for the summer. This restaurant was a favorite of the tourists, aka Bennies. We'd have a dozen waitresses on, even on the weekdays. We'd often do over a thousand dinners in a night. At the end of our shifts, the waitresses would refill the ketchup bottles, salt & pepper shakers, and were allowed to have coleslaw and chowder. The cooks, dishwashers and bus boys could have a meal if they liked. So, on my last night before going back to college, my friend and I decided to hide in the walk-in refrigerator and have a piece of cheesecake. That was a big no-no. The kitchen was still bustling when I took one of the pieces of cheesecake and smooshed it in my friend's face. She had an incredibly loud and distinctive laugh. She laughed so hard that our manager could hear her from the other side of the kitchen. He opened the walk-in door and there we were. Me with an empty cheesecake plate and my friend with cheesecake all over her face. He fired us both.

I wasn't too upset about being fired because I was going back to college, but my friend needed her job through the winter. So, the next morning we came back to the restaurant and begged the manager for our jobs back. He hired us again. That night the owner, Jack Baker, found out about it and fired us again.

While in college, I worked two summers as a toll collector on the Garden State Parkway at the Asbury Park Plaza. A bunch of college kids worked with me. It didn't take long to figure out that we wanted to be assigned to the south bound lanes on a Friday night. All the Bennies were coming down to the Shore and likely had beer in their cars. It was especially likely if they were pulling a boat. The tolls were 25 cents then and when a suspected beer hauler came through our lanes, we'd offer a free toll in exchange for a beer. By the end of night, we'd have dozens of beers in our booth. Ah, the good old days of beer-for-tolls and toll booth shenanigans. "Benny Bingo."

Our shift would end at 11pm, just in time to hit the bars with friends. After having hundreds of people going through my lane each night, everyone at the bar looked familiar to me; looked like I'd met them before. It drove me crazy!

During a daytime shift, a school bus came through. The driver paid the toll and as the bus pulled out of the lane, a kid through a big chunk of tire rubber at me and hit me in the face. In a flash, I turned my booth light to red and started running down the Parkway after the bus. The driver must have seen me running like a lunatic and pulled over. I got on the bus and pointed out the little shit to the driver. I then ran back down the Parkway, against traffic, and got back in my booth.

Sometimes we'd get assigned to one of the exit ramps. Typically, just two people. My co-worker would stuff the automated toll basket with a sock. The drivers would pull through and throw their quarter, but the light wouldn't turn green. He and I would just waive the people through and every hour or so we'd empty out the basket filled with quarters.

In my Junior year of college at Glassboro State, 3 friends and I had just moved into a 2-bedroom off-campus house. It was one of our first night's there and a terrible storm moved through. Three of us went to bed and the fourth fell asleep on the couch. At 3am we heard a curdling scream coming from the living room. I ran out of my bedroom and in the darkness, I could see a man running out the front door. My friend was screaming that the man held his hand over her mouth, laid on top of her and said, "if you make a sound, I'll kill you!" My friend could see that he had a gun. Screaming may not have been her best decision given the circumstances, but the outcome was good. We called the police who took a report. They suggested that the next morning we hang underpants and bras on the clothesline to give the appearance we were still in the house and that we should leave the house because there had been rapes in the neighborhood. They would then stakeout the house to see if he'd return. It was tough because school was just beginning, and we really didn't have anywhere to go. Two of us rented an apartment, one moved in with friends and the fourth moved back home.

The police apprehended the man, who lived in the neighborhood. It turned out he was the teenage son of the Chief of Police. And the gun was the Chief's. We learned that the police had suspected this guy early on and the night he came into our house, the cops had called the Chief and asked him to check if his son's clothes were wet. He told them "Nope, he's bone dry."

CHAPTER TWO – OUT INTO THE REAL WORLD

Right out of college, I got a job working at the Golden Nugget in Atlantic City. I commuted from Point Pleasant Beach each day, about an hour and 15 minutes each way. Employees of the casinos could park along Route 40 approaching AC and take a shuttle bus into the city. I preferred to drive all the way in and take my chances parking on the street. The neighborhood folks didn't like that I was parking there and, unbeknownst to me, put sugar in my gas tank. That night, after working a 4pm – midnight shift, as I drove north on the Garden State Parkway, my car shuddered and stalled. I pulled over and waited a few minutes, started it back up and went on my way. This happened every ten miles or so. A State Trooper pulled over during one stop. I explained what was happening and he got back in his Troop car. The next time I stopped, the same Trooper pulled over and told me "you can't keep going like this. Let's get you to the barracks and see if we can have someone pick you up." I grabbed my backpack from my car and as we entered the barracks, the Trooper patted the backpack and said "Ah, a sixer!" I was scared to death. I had a six pack of beer in the backpack. I wasn't drinking it, but it seemed somehow illegal to carry one into a police barracks. It was now 3am and I was able to get in touch with my brother, Stephen. We agreed to meet in Brick where the Trooper would drop me off. We still had 2 hours to kill. So, the Trooper pulled into an empty picnic area on the Parkway and said, "why don't you crack open that sixer?" So, the two of us sat in the front seat of the Troop car and split a 6 pack.

One of my favorite jobs was working at WADB Radio in Belmar, NJ. It was in the early '80's. I was a copywriter and often produced the commercials. I made $8,000 a year. The station manager became a friend and announced one afternoon that she had fired the overnight on-air announcer. She told me she and I were going to take his shift. So, from midnight to 8am, we misread the barometric pressure, mispronounced the middle eastern city names we read from the Associated Press feed, and laughed out loud way too many times.

In my mid-twenties, I got a job working as a management consultant in downtown Manhattan. I was a clam digger, out of my element. I trusted everyone. One morning walking to my job at Citibank, I stood on the corner with lots of people waiting for the light to change. The woman next to me was holding a green canvas bank bag. She said

"I just found this bag and it's filled with money. I don't know what to do." I said, "well open it." She did and pulled out a stack of hundred-dollar bills and a note that read "enclosed is $98,000 US dollars for the purpose of Iranian tax evasion." She quickly stuffed the money and note back into the bag. I said "Oh my God! What are you going to do?" She said "well this is newfound money for me. I'd be happy to split it with you." I said in disbelief "but you don't even know me!" As we crossed the street, another woman joined us. The first woman said "I'm scared to split it on the street. There's a diner right down this alley where we can go. It will be safer." I started to walk down the alley with these women thinking "$54,000 or late for work?" My gut told me something wasn't right, and I turned and quickly walked away. The women started screaming and cursing at me. I got to Citibank and told the supervisor, my client, what had happened. She was a seasoned New Yorker. I was like "Gidget Goes to

Manhattan." As I told her the story, she had kind of a blank look on her face like I was some kind of an idiot. Here I was the consultant. I was supposed to be the smart one. She calmly explained to me that the women would not split the money with me but would ask for a few thousand dollars in "good faith". "There was no money" she said, "there was likely one fake hundred-dollar bill on either side of the stack, with blank paper in between." I then had to go about my day, with very little credibility, instructing her how to streamline workflow and improve efficiencies.

While working in Manhattan, I commuted 2-1/2 hours from Point Pleasant Beach. It became too much, so I got a studio apartment in Jersey City. I had to fix up the apartment a bit. I was painting the inside of my casement window, perched up on the ledge. It was dark out, I was on the 3rd floor, with no balcony. I suddenly saw a man staring into the window, just inches from me. I screamed, threw the paint brush, and rolled onto the couch. It took a minute, but I realized that the man was the reflection of my Honeymooner's tee shirt with Ralph Kramden's face in the moon.

While still living in Jersey City, I met my Mom and Dad at an Irish dance in West Orange. I often went to these events with them. I have a deep connection to my Irish heritage and love Irish music. On the way home, I hit a deep pothole, but made it home. I knew I'd probably have a flat tire in the morning, which I did. Stupidly, I had parked on a street with a slight incline. So, every time I jacked up the car, it would slide off. After two tries, a guy came by and said, "What you needs is a cinder block." "Yes! That's a great idea" I said. And the two of us started looking through yards for a cinder block. In a minute or two, I saw the man jogging up the block. "Maybe he realized where there's a cinder block" I thought. So, I stood and had a cigarette waiting for him to come back. He didn't. So, I finally was able to jack the car up and change the tire. I was on my way to Brooklyn to visit my new friend I'd made at work. This was in the mid 1980's, so there were no cell phones and no way for me to let her know I'd be late. This was also before GPS, and I got lost going to her apartment. Eventually I found it. When she answered the door, she didn't say hi, just asked where my wallet was. "Right here" I said opening my purse. No wallet. Apparently, the cinder block guy went into my car and stole my wallet. Of course, I'd left both doors open being the naive clam digger I was. In my wallet was a piece of paper with some old friends' phone numbers. So, after the bad guy ditched my wallet, whoever found it started calling those numbers. They reached a high school friend who then called my sister, who then called my Brooklyn friend. By then I was two hours late getting there, so everyone imagined me dead in a ditch.

In the mid-1980's, my Dad, brother, two cousins and I went to Ireland together. I was 25 and my brother and cousins were 21. I got to be the designated driver of a minivan we'd rented. It wasn't at all what we expected. It was a commercial van with no carpeting, just a metal floor and a 3-foot-tall stick shift. In Ireland they drive on the left side of the road. That was hard enough but I also had to shift with my left hand. Driving down the country road dodging the sheep was no easy feat.

We headed west to spend the day on the Inishmore, the largest island of the Aran Islands. It was a two-hour boat ride from Ballaveere. The Aran Islands were then the only place left in Ireland where Irish Gaelic is the primary language. The island was just as it was hundreds of years ago. The only businesses on the island were Joe Mac's Pub, St. Kevin's B&B and Joe Watty's Pub. We arrived on

Inishmore and checked into St. Kevin's B&B. After checking in, we took a horse and buggy ride and saw an ancient cemetery with headstones dating back 1200 years. Many O'Flaherty's lie there. They occupied the West of Ireland for hundreds of years and left their mark. On the Isle of Inishere, a smaller Aran Island, stands O'Brien's Castle, a 15th century fort built by the O'Brien's who ruled the island until they were defeated by the O'Flaherty's in 1585.

We were to check out and head back to Ballaveere the next morning, but the weather had turned bad. It was pouring rain and the sea had turned rough. We'd have to stay another night. We spent the morning in the B&B writing a song we'd later call the Aran Islands. My cousin was a great guitar player and my brother and I could sing. After lunch we decided to head up the hill to Joe Watty's pub. We brought the guitar and met a bunch of Irish kids who also had guitars. We spent hours playing Irish songs and they played American songs. Throughout the day, we probably played the Aran Islands song several times. It was growing dark, so we decided to head down the hill to Joe Mac's pub. There was no indoor plumbing in the pubs, so we had to stand in line for an outhouse. There were a couple of Irish girls in front of me and I overheard one say in her lovely brogue "We don't have to go up to Joe Watty's. The Americans are on their way down, and they're gonna play that song for us!" We wound up playing our song a couple of times in Joe Mac's, and by the end of night we had the whole pub singing the song we'd written that morning.

After returning from the Aran Islands, Dad dropped us at the entrance of The International Hotel in Shannon while he parked. We entered the lobby and saw just one other person there…Maureen O'Hara. My cousin immediately began his best impression of John Wayne. He put his arms out from his sides and sauntered toward her saying in his best John Wayne voice "Maureen, it's good ta see ya." She skedaddled to the elevator.

CHAPTER 3 – BLIND DATES GONE WRONG

Before I was married, my good friend set me up with a teacher with whom she worked. We went to dinner at The Ark in Point Pleasant Beach. We were having some nice conversation when I crossed my leg and clunked into something. I knew it wasn't the table leg. What the heck was it? I looked under the table and saw nothing but my date's legs. He said "Oh, sorry, that's my wooden leg."

I married in 1993 to a State Trooper. We had two kids, Conor and Molly. My loves. My ex and I had good jobs, a lovely home, and rarely argued. I thought things were great. One night he said, "I think it's time we move on." I said, "Where we goin'?" He was asking for a divorce. Our kids were only 3 and 6 at the time. I was heartbroken. But the kids and I managed. I was able to give them a good life. Now I have two amazing adults. No regrets!

Not long after my divorce, my good friend called me and said "I have someone for you. But there's a catch. He's got a giant hook nose and a glass eye." I said "for real? Okay, you can give him my number." So "giant hook nose, glass eye" and I went for a drink at Marlins in Bay Head. He seemed like a nice guy. He had long hair and liked to roller blade. At one point he said "you know what I like to do sometimes? I like to take my eye out, place it on the bar and say, 'Here's lookin' at ya." There wasn't a second date with "giant hook nose, glass eye." About 6 months later, a bunch of girlfriends and I went to a gay bar in Asbury Park called George's. It was karaoke night. There up on the stage was "giant hook nose, glass eye" in a polyester dress and sensible shoes singing "Santa Baby."

Another blind date. We met for dinner and started the usual chit chatting about ourselves. Everything seemed to be going well until he ordered a large plate of spicy wings. As we were eating, I noticed his face was turning red and he was starting to sweat. I asked if he was okay, and he replied that the wings were much spicier than he had anticipated. Suddenly, he jumped up from the table and ran to the restroom. I could hear him vomiting loudly from across the restaurant. After a few minutes, he came back to the table looking embarrassed and disheveled. To make matters worse, his nose started to bleed profusely. He had apparently burst a blood vessel from the strain of vomiting. I felt badly for him; he was so mortified that he asked for the check, apologized, and left the restaurant.

Match.com has become less of a place to find love and more of a place to get a great story. I met a Match date at the River House in Brielle, NJ. It was a lovely restaurant overlooking the Manasquan River. We met for dinner. He did the ordering. He ordered one small appetizer for us to split. That was it. After dinner, I felt badly sending him on his way because he'd driven 2 hours to get there. He had never been to Point Pleasant Beach, so I asked him if he'd like to take a walk on the boardwalk. So, we walked, taking in all the great smells of food. We got to the end of the boardwalk, and he asked, "what do you want to do now?" I felt like saying "I want to go home and get something to eat." But I didn't. He said, "I have a convertible Mazda Miata, do you want to take a ride?" I felt like saying "no" but I didn't. He explained that he was a member of the Mazda Miata Club and that he would often go on road trips with other club members just riding through the hills together. So we went for a ride, my hair blowing in the wind, my stomach growling." That was the end of Mazda Miata Man.

Two weeks after my date with Mazda Miata Man, I had another Match date. We met at The Cabin in Freehold. To break the ice with this guy, I decided to tell him my Mazda Miata Guy story. He looked at me blankly and said "didn't you see the picture of me on my Match profile standing in front of my Mazda Miata? I'm a club member too."

Another Match.com connection. I spoke with Michael on the phone for over an hour before agreeing to meet him for drinks. He lived about 45 minutes south of me, so I suggested a halfway point, Houlihan's. He agreed. Not long after hanging up, Michael called back and said "Here's what I'm gonna do. I'm gonna take a bus to Point Pleasant Beach and meet you there. I googled hotels there and found one on Arnold Avenue. You don't have to stay with me, but if my sister, who lives in Sayreville, can't pick me up after the date, I'll stay at the hotel." I said "Okay if that's what you want to do. Am I picking you up at the bus station?" "Yes" he said. And we hung up. When we first spoke, Michael was eager to let me know what a successful career he had. That really wasn't that important to me, but I thought "Does this guy even have a car?" So, I called him back and asked if he had a car. He explained that three years ago his daughter needed a car, and he gave his to her. I asked if he had a driver's license. He texted me a picture of an expired Massachusetts license. I told him he was full of shit. To somehow prove he was legit, he texted me a picture of a tax return from 8 years earlier showing he'd made $215,000. So, Michael and I had our first fight without even meeting. The next night I was out to dinner with the girls and told them the story. They wanted to see a picture of him. I brought his Match.com profile picture up, forgetting that the person is alerted when that happens. I immediately got a text from him saying "Ah, ya miss me already!"

My blind dates have a way of ending in completely unexpected ways. I once met a date for dinner. I ate my meal at what I thought was a reasonable pace. I was done with my dinner when my date hadn't even made a dent in his. The conversation was kind of boring, so I was looking to get out of there. He didn't finish his dinner for another hour. Finally, we got up from the table and headed for the door. I was thanking him as we walked but realized he was yards behind me. I waited until he caught up and we walked to the parking lot. I walk fast, but this guy was crawling along. Finally, we hugged and kissed goodbye but something was wrong. I still had my arms around him as he began to fall backwards. I held onto him and the two of us crumpled to the ground. He said "I'm sorry. I had my hip replaced." I said "When, this morning?"

I had another date at a local restaurant called B2. We ordered dinner and drinks and had some nice conversation. Bob was an interesting guy. He had consulted for Chase Bank many years ago and was tasked with lowering their operating expenses. He did a study on how much it cost the bank for a customer to deposit a check. He then suggested that the bank let the customers make their own deposits with their phones. He explained that the technology was already there. They just needed to take a picture of the check and submit it through the bank's app. Pretty cool! So, about halfway through dinner, Bob suddenly stopped talking to me. The hostess came by and asked how dinner was, but he didn't answer. He was eating very slowly and seemed catatonic. I was nervous; I didn't know what was wrong. I knew Bob had a daughter, so I asked him for her cell number, thinking maybe she could shed some light. At first, he wouldn't give it to me, but finally I was able to call her. I started explaining what was happening and she immediately told me he was in a diabetic coma. The hostess got him some orange juice and called an ambulance. Now, here I am on a blind date surrounded by 3 cops and 2 EMT's, with ambulance lights flashing into the restaurant. One police officer came to me with his note pad asking my husband's name. I explained that we were on a blind date and that I didn't even know his last name. Eventually the orange juice worked, and Bob was back to normal.

Another date gone wrong. We met at Frankie's in Point Pleasant Beach for drinks. He texted me that he was there and asked that I text him when I got to the parking lot.

Hmmmm. I guess that's gentlemanly. Nice. I got there and texted him. He came out to the parking lot and went in for a big hug and a kiss on the lips. Mind you this is our first meeting. I gave him a quick cheek and we went inside. We had some nice conversation, though a red flag did appear. He didn't have a house or an apartment. He lived with his adult daughter. Ok, not the end of the world. We sat for about an hour and a half. In that time, he had four cocktails, plus whatever he had before I got there. It was time to go, and he walked me to my car. He started kissing me goodnight and before I knew it his tongue was jammed down my throat. I felt like I was back in 8th grade. I couldn't get in the car fast enough.

I had a blind date scheduled for drinks at Harrigan's in Sea Girt, NJ. We explained to each other what we'd be wearing so we could recognize each other. My date said

"Look for me. I'll be at the bar with a black turtleneck and a grey sweater." I got to the bar and spotted him immediately. I sat next to him, and we introduced ourselves. We talked about where we were from, what things we like to do for fun and so on. We were getting along nicely but he suddenly said "I'm sorry, I have to go. I have to meet someone." I was taken aback because I thought it was going well. At that moment I looked across the bar and there was a man with a black turtleneck and grey sweater sheepishly waiving at me.

The Midget Dentist. I know that is no longer an acceptable description of anyone, but back in the old days, we were allowed to say something like that. I had a Match.com date with a very short dentist. He wasn't an actual midget. I'd say he was 5'0" even though his profile said he was 5'4". He picked me up for dinner in his huge SUV. As he climbed into the driver's side, I wasn't sure he was going to make it. He was grabbing onto the door and the truck seat, pulling himself up into the truck. As we started down the road, I couldn't help but laugh to myself at the site of him holding onto the steering wheel with his arms stretched out so he could reach the 10 and 2 position. Being so small, he couldn't see over the steering wheel and had to look *through* the steering wheel. We made it to the restaurant where we had some nice conversation. However, once the discussion turned to his ex-wife, he started to well up. I asked what was wrong. "I miss her so much," he said. Now the tears started streaming down. I tried to console him but didn't quite know what to say. Another blind date gone sideways.

Here's another one. My date arranged for us to go to a Giants game. I love football and was really looking forward to it. As we sat in the stands, I noticed this seagull dive bombing the area around us. He'd come swooping down, very close to us, then fly away. This went on for quite a while. I don't know what made me think this, but I was sure he was going to drop a load on me. Sure enough, as he came swooping down, the bird shit came flying toward me and splattered on my sweater. The whole crowd around me had seen it coming and when it hit me, let out a collective "ahhhhhh."

CHAPTER 4: WHAT ARE THE ODDS OF THAT?

I was in Frank's Arcade on the Point Pleasant Beach boardwalk with Molly and her friends. I put my keys down on the ticket counter and turned away. In an instant, my keys were gone. I looked all around the counter but no luck. I went about the pain in the ass process of getting new keys. About 6 months later, my friend called and asked if I lost my keys. I said I was pretty sure they were stolen, but yes. He said his daughter was skiing with friends in New Hampshire. She was riding in the back seat, looked down and saw keys with Molly's 4th grade picture on them. My keys! Now let's go back 25 years before that to 1983 at the Raritan rest area on the Garden State Parkway. It was midafternoon as I was leaving the rest area there was a beautiful young man in a suit who was hitchhiking. Of course, as everyone did back then, I picked him up. I asked why he was hitchhiking, and he explained that his Mercedes had broken down. He said he lived with his in-laws in Mantoloking, a beautiful, affluent shore town just a couple of miles south of me. I told him I'd be happy to drive him all the way home. On that ride we talked about our jobs. I was working at the Golden Nugget in Atlantic City, and he was starting a new magazine called "Dining Out." I told him I'd gone to college for marketing and advertising. In that 45-minute ride he convinced me to quit my job and come work for him. We'd be selling ad space to Jersey Shore restaurants, and I'd get a 50% commission. So that following week I quit my job and started riding all over Monmouth and Ocean counties selling ad space with him. Oddly, we had to use my car because his was still in the shop. I had the opportunity to meet his wife and in-laws at their spectacular ocean front home and even attended a christening party for his son.

Over time, with him collecting down payment checks from restauranteurs and me collecting no pay or gas money, I realized that there was no magazine. After two months, I quit and got a job as assistant marketing director at Woodbridge Mall. I had a visit from the editor of the *real* "Dining Out" magazine who was trying to sell ad space to the mall. I asked him if he knew John Berry. He said "Sure, I put him in jail!" Now here's the fun part. The young man who was driving the car where my keys were found was the son of John Berry, the child whose christening party I attended. He had worked at the arcade and swiped the keys hoping he might be able to steal stuff from my car. He never found the car and tossed the keys in his backseat.

Super Storm Sandy 2012 at the Jersey Shore was devastating. We were lucky to be 5 blocks from the beach, but everyone up to 4 blocks from the beach suffered terrible damage to their homes and cars. We had no power for 9 days. Molly was 15 at the time, living home. Conor was away at Temple University. We had a portable generator that kept the fridge running, but gasoline was impossible to find locally. Fortunately, Sam, our new neighbor worked an hour away in Trenton and could bring back gas. We ran an extension cord over the fence so he and his wife, Darleen, could run their fridge and some lights. We really didn't know them well but when they invited us over for dinner, we accepted. I brought over one of those big bottles of wine and as I'm opening it asked, "who would like some wine?" "Oh, not Darleen," said Sam. "When Darleen drinks, really horrible things happen!" he laughed. So, no wine for Darleen. After about an hour, the bottle was empty, so I sent Molly back home to get another bottle. She came back with two of the big bottles, much more than we needed. We had a nice dinner and returned home. We went to bed around 9 because when there's no power, it's boring and I could only take so many of nights having Molly perform her standup comedy act for me with a broom as a microphone. Later that night, I was awoken to a cackling sound in my bedroom. I pulled off my Zsa Zsa's and there was Darleen! I said "Darleen, DID YOU DRINK THE WINE??" She said "Yes, whahahahaha!" and she flung herself into my bed! I jumped out of bed and took her by the shoulders and led her to the guest room. I told her to stay there, and I'd see her in the morning. Darleen had never been in my house before which is a big, 5-bedroom home, so I'm guessing she had to wander around a while to find me. The next morning, Darleen was gone, but her orange sneakers were left behind. I told Molly I was going next store to drop them off and she said "Ohhhhh, I am NOT gonna miss this!" So, we rang the bell, and Darleen answered. I was holding up her orange sneakers. She had a look that told us she, at first, had no recollection of what happened. Then, slowly, we could see it was coming back to her. We let her off the hook and never discussed it again.

Sam was about 10 years younger than me. A good-looking guy who liked to invite himself over on a regular basis. He would walk in the backyard by the pool and if he couldn't find me, he'd come in the back door and call my name. Sometimes if I didn't want to see him, I'd hide on the front porch. One day I was lying by the pool and Sam came over and asked me if I wanted to do shots with him. It was 11am. I said no thanks, but that didn't stop him. We talked for about 2 hours about nothing in particular. He finally left and went into his yard. At that point, two utility company workers were entering my yard to pick up an old refrigerator from the garage. At the very moment they were passing the fence between our yards, Sam peeked through the fence and said in a drunken way "If you want to come over and lie naked, it's okay with me!"

My friend had an early morning delivery to her home. She had just showered and was dressed only in her robe. She opened the front door where the delivery man was and stepped out onto the porch. Her dog decided the door should be closed, so he jumped up onto it and slammed it shut. The door was locked. The delivery man helped her pull a ladder over from the side of the house so she could climb up and crawl through a second story window. She got halfway up the ladder, as he held it steady below, and a gust of wind blew her robe wide open. "Don't look!" she yelled to the delivery man. Next, she sees three cop cars, lights flashing, coming up to her house. The alarm had been tripped. All before 7:30 am!

Conor, Molly, and I were on vacation in Cancun and on our way back home at the airport. They asked for our visas, which I couldn't find. We were instructed to go into the bowels of the airport to an office where there were several other nitwits who had lost their visas. We were told we had to take a bus to a specific bank and purchase new visas. We had only an hour and a half before our flight. We got to the bank where there was only one teller and about 10 people ahead of us. I overheard someone say they don't take credit cards, only cash. I knew I had very little cash left after a week's vacation. Each visa was $50. I asked the kids to search their pockets for money. We came up with only $50. Suddenly, the man behind us handed me a $100 bill. I couldn't believe it! I fumbled to find paper and a pen to get his name and address to repay him. I thanked him profusely for being so kind. As he wrote down his info, I noticed a Claddagh ring on his finger. "Well, it's got to be an Irish name!" I laughed. He said it was and wrote down Kevin Kelly, 16 Borden Ave, Neptune, NJ. I said "are you kidding? I live in Point Pleasant Beach!" He laughed and asked if I knew Kelly's Tavern. Of course, I did. It was an iconic Irish bar at the Jersey Shore. I'd spent many an evening there. He said, "I'm one of the owners!"

Molly and I were in Fort Lauderdale at a hotel getting ready for a cruise the next day. I decided to go for a run in the morning. I came back to the hotel, through the lobby to 4th floor. I knocked on the door, but Molly didn't answer. I called her and told her I was at the door. She said "No, you're not. I'm standing right here, and I don't see you." I looked around and noticed that the carpeting looked different. I was in the wrong hotel.

The house developed a terrible stink. I assumed something had died in the walls. Maybe a squirrel or a racoon and that the stench would eventually dissipate. But it went on for two weeks. Molly, now 25, would walk around the house gagging. I assumed she was being dramatic. It smelled pretty bad, but I don't have a great sense of smell. The smell seemed to be coming from the basement, near the furnace chimney that ran from the furnace, up through 4 floors and out the roof. Finally, Molly couldn't take it anymore and called a chimney sweep. They said it would be $135 to remove anything that didn't belong in the chimney. Great. When the workers went into the basement to begin the job, one of them ran out of house and vomited in the driveway. Suddenly they were all wearing bandanas around their faces. When the sweep was done, they said there weren't any animals in the chimney and asked if I knew what was in the basement freezer. Conor had brought home a 20-pound turkey at Thanksgiving that we saved for another time. Unbeknownst to us, the freezer had broken, and the turkey was rotting. I don't think I've had to deal with anything so disgusting as cleaning out the freezer where an inch of turkey guts was rotting on the bottom of the freezer. In the meantime, the chimney sweep guys said I needed a new chimney cap and liner. Now I had a $5,000 turkey.

I was at a work conference in Orlando. The president of one of the country's largest equipment/tool distributors was up on stage touting the company's new app with voice recognition. In front of a thousand people or so and a giant jumbotron, he took out his phone and opened the app. He explained you could search any item by voice. He put the phone to his mouth and said, "20 Pound Compressor." Up on the jumbotron, in giant letters appeared "20 Pound Pussy."

Molly and I went to St. Maarten when she was 10 years old. We stayed on the Dutch side near the airport. Our hotel was right next to where the planes come in for landings. There was a small beach right before the runway and the planes would come in low, so low it seemed like you could reach up and touch them. People regularly would stand on that little beach waiting for planes and would sometimes get blown into the air and land in the water from the backdraft.

One day we decided to go to a beach on the French side of St. Maarten. It was a topless beach. Molly couldn't stop laughing about it. She kept bothering me to take off my top. She was relentless. So, finally I said we could go out into the sea and take off our bathing suit tops. She didn't even have boobs yet, but she thought it was hysterical. As we're walking out of the water, here comes a family from Point Pleasant Beach. Mom, dad and two kids. I was on the Board of Education at the time and all I could imagine was the local paper headline reading "Board of Ed President Spotted Frolicking Topless."

My good friend is crazy about dogs. One day she was driving down a busy, local road and saw an Irish Setter wandering around the roadside with no owner in sight. She followed the dog through side streets and eventually got out of her van and chased the dog to a front lawn and tackled him. She put him in her van and brought him home. She saw he had a license on his collar and called the Point Pleasant authorities to get the address of the owner. As she drove through town, she was getting closer to the area in which she found him. Finally, she reached the address and realized she had stolen the dog from his own front lawn!

Each year I give the sanitation workers and the mail carrier a check at holiday time. I leave the card and check for the mail carrier in the mailbox, and I tape the card to the top of the trashcan for the sanitation guys. One year, I saw that the sanitation gift was no longer on the lid of the trashcan, though they had not yet picked up the garbage. It wasn't a lot of money, but it irked me that someone had taken it. I went to the police station, and they were able to get the video of the check being cashed. There he was…my mail carrier. So, the mailman stole the garbage man's check.

I have a good friend from high school who is wonderfully innocent and funny. Most of the time when we're all laughing, we're laughing at her. And she's laughing the hardest. Once, in high school, she said "Mt. Rushmore is amazing. How in the world did the wind create something that turned out to look just like those presidents?"

I was walking on the boardwalk and came to the Manasquan inlet. There was a young man sitting on the bench. As I looked out over the inlet, my intuition was telling me something was wrong. It was a powerful feeling. After a minute or two, I was compelled to ask him "are you okay?" He looked at me, a little surprised that I would ask, and said "yes." I went on my way, and that night I saw a "missing child" alert on NBC. It was him. I called the hotline and reported that I'd seen him. I first prayed that he'd be returned to his family, but then realized that that might not be the best course for him. Maybe he wants to be missing for good reasons.

I was on a plane with my little 5-pound Maltipoo, Quigley, heading to see Conor in Charlotte where he had moved after getting his first job after college at Aramark. A woman across the aisle was talking about spending the weekend with her son who had just graduated and moved from Jersey to Charlotte in July as well. We had a nice conversation during the flight. She was enamored with Quigley and even asked if she could hold him. When we landed, she asked if she could take a picture of Quigley. The next day, Conor and I were at a festival in Charlotte. There were about 1000 people there. Really crowded. We wandered around trying to find a seat at one of the picnic tables and saw empty spots at one. I asked the woman if it was okay if we sat there. She looked at us and yelled "is that Quigley?!!!" Yep, same woman.

When Molly was 25, she went to Nepal for a few weeks to teach science and soccer to the orphaned Nepali kids at an American camp. Her trip there was one for the books. She flew from Newark, NJ to Istanbul. From there to

Katmandu. The 3rd leg was to be to where the school is in the Himalayas. That flight hit monsoon-like weather and was diverted to a different airport where they dumped her off with her luggage and gave her no help in getting to the school. A lovely Nepali man, who was also traveling to that area, helped her by getting them a rickshaw. They rode in the pouring rain and found a van that was going in the right direction. Eighteen people piled into the van which held twelve. As they drove through the mountains, they frequently had to get out and clear the roadway from the mudslide debris. Molly saw a cliff to her left and frightening mudslides to her right. She cried thinking this might be the end for her. Finally, a rockslide came down and completely blocked the road. They had to get out of the van and gather their luggage. Molly, 5/1" 100 pounds, pulled her duffle bag filled with soccer balls and her suitcases up and over the rockpile, still in the monsoon rains. A school bus was able to come and get her and bring her to the school. When she arrived, she found that there were cockroaches in her room, including her bed. As awful as the journey was, she loved the camp. Life changing. The kids were so kind and loving toward one another. They had literally nothing but were the happiest kids she'd ever met.

CHAPTER 5 – MORE PRETTY GOOD STORIES

I have a good friend named Patty. I've gotten a lot of joy out of driving her crazy. Whenever we'd go food shopping, I would point out various foods to her and say things like "Hamburger, Patty!" "Patty, Cake!" "Rice, Patty!" She was never quite as amused as me.

Like most dogs, my dog Quigley will make swimming motions with the legs when he's held over water. We held him over the pool water, and he'd start swimming. Then we held him over his water bowl, and he'd start swimming. Finally, we held him over a shot glass of water and, yep, he'd start swimming.

Molly and her friend waiting for me while I checked out at Home Depot.

Thanksgiving of her Junior year in college, Molly sent me this text.

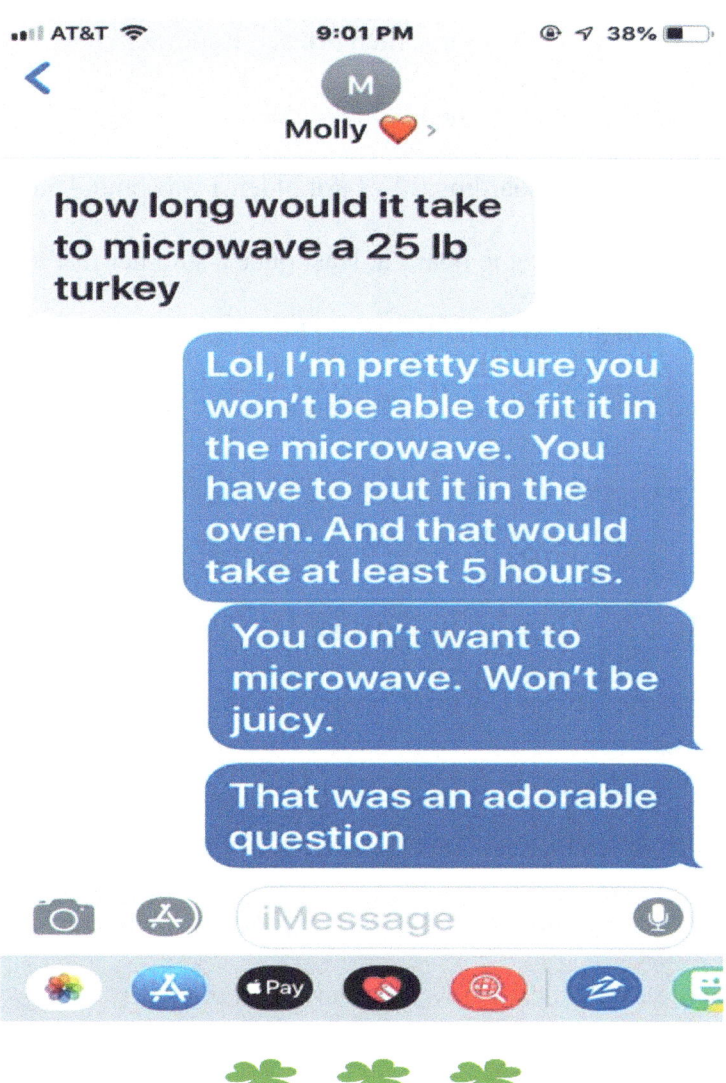

Old broads shouldn't boogie board. I love the beach. It's my favorite place to be. I've spent many a beautiful day there with a friend group called "Beach Buddies." It's typically 3-4 hours of non-stop laughter. For many years, I enjoyed boogie boarding. As I got older, I was bound and determined to boogie board at least once a summer just to prove I could still do it. Recently, I was out there with a friend who wanted to prove herself as well. We strapped the leashes on our wrists and ventured out into the waves. The first wave was one I had to dive under as I wasn't going to be able to get to it in time. As I dove under, the wave took the boogie board with a lot of force and snapped my arm back. I heard a crack and knew that couldn't be good. When I came out of the water, it really didn't hurt. But as the minutes went by, I knew something was wrong. Maybe I'd dislocated my shoulder, I thought. I drove myself to the emergency room and got x-rays. I had broken my shoulder. Ugh. I was given a sling and told to visit an orthopedic doctor. Three days after the accident, and still in the sling, I figured I could still do some of my exercising, like power walking. I set out on a 2 mile walk and as I was crossing the railroad tracks, I tripped on a track and went face down in an instant. As I lay there, I immediately thought of those 1960's cartoons with the damsel lying on the railroad tracks with rope tied around her chest and legs. I was mortified and jumped right up noting that not one soul driving by bothered to stop and help me.

I won my ex-husband's cousins in the divorce. They had two kids a little older than mine and lived in North Jersey. In the summers, they'd come down and stay for the weekends. They are Italian, so they were in charge of the food. I am Irish, so I was in charge of the booze. It was a perfect fit. At one visit they gave me a gift that was a sign that read "BED & BREAKFAST - YOU MAKE BOTH."

In college, Molly would often text me asking for a picture of Quigley. I would always respond with a picture of me and a little sliver of Quigs.

I've noticed that our sweet customer service folks have a very hard time saying goodbye to us. Rep: "Is there anything else I can help you with?" Me: "No, thanks for your help." Rep: "Of course. It's my aim to provide you with excellent service." Me: "Thanks and have a good day." Rep: "Have I resolved all of your issues?" Me: "Yes, thanks so much." Rep: "Stay safe and thanks for being a valued customer." Me: "Have a great day." Rep: "I hope you have a great day too." Me: "Bye-bye." Rep: "Thanks for being a valued customer. Bye-bye." Whew...

When I worked in IT at Goldman Sachs, I was assigned a Y2K compliance job. I was to travel to traders' offices all over the world to make sure that their computers would survive the rollover into the year 2000. Any code that they had in their software that referenced a date likely started with the number "19" and wouldn't recognize 2000. So, the software had to be modified. I went to some locations in the U.S. and to Monte Carlo, Malta, Hawaii, and Tokyo. My kids were 4 and 1 at the time, so I would go to each location for a one-hour meeting and come back that day or the next cause I thought my kids would be missing me. I could have parlayed the trips into several days if I wanted to. I don't even think the kids knew I was gone. Anyway, while visiting Tokyo I was struck by how everyone follows the rules. For example, if you're standing on a corner waiting for the light to turn green, you stand there whether there are cars coming or not. Very strange. There could be 20 or 30 people standing on the corner with no cars coming and they'd wait. In the morning, from my hotel window, I looked down to the street and saw a pickup truck passing by with dozens of cases of what looked like beer in the bed of the truck. It hit a bump and several cases fell off the truck which then continued down the street. It was rush hour, so there were lots of pedestrians passing by and no one seemed to bother with the beer. I thought "jeez, if this was New York, people would be scooping up those beers and stashing them in their brief cases and purses." After a couple of minutes, people did start coming out to the street and collecting the beers. "Well maybe we're not so different" I thought. They were picking up the bottles, putting them back in the cases, and stacking them on the side of the street presumably for the driver to retrieve.

As a management consultant at a client's corporate office, I'm supposed to be dressed professionally. I sometimes miss that mark.

I was invited to a sex toy party. Having grown up Irish Catholic, it was a little cringy for me, but I agreed to go. Part of the festivities included making up a "sexy" name for myself which included my actual first name, writing it on a name tag, and sticking it on my chest. I had to leave a little early because I had a meeting at borough hall. I was on the Endowment Committee along with the mayor, some council members, and a few other residents. I arrived at the meeting, sat down, and could feel the stares. I had forgotten to take off my "Cum On Eileen" name tag.

A friend of mine came along with me to the Hair Salon. As she sat waiting, reading a magazine, she came over to me and showed me a picture of a young woman's haircut. "You should get this haircut. You'll look just like her!" she said. I said, "You mean my teeth will be straight?"

I've grown up around the water my whole life. A few years ago, I heard about a boat club that was like a timeshare for boats. It's a great concept. You buy into the club, and you have access to several different boats. They have bowriders, pontoon boats, and center consoles. You simply reserve a boat for a day, half day or even just a couple of hours. I already had my boating license, so I was all set. I took lots of friends and family out with me, usually for a happy hour on the water. We would cruise around the Manasquan River, out through the Point

Pleasant Canal to the bay, and through the Inlet to the ocean. My friends and family would have a great time having cocktails, listening to music, and taking in the beautiful surroundings. But a pattern was starting to develop. I ran aground more than once. I attempted to go under the railroad track bridge without enough room and broke off the GPS from the top of the boat. After the outings, the boat club staff would dock the boat for you, which was the hardest part of being a captain. Mid-season, however, the boat club changed the rules and made members dock the boats themselves. This is when I was dubbed "Captain Crunch." I came in too fast and cracked the motor cover by hitting the dock. As much as I loved being out on a boat, I didn't love being the Captain. It was too stressful! I was responsible for these lives! And everyone was having fun but me. I lasted two seasons as Captain Crunch, then turned in my captain's hat and boat shoes.

There were a few years when we had an usually large number of possums around the yard. Our beagle, Sadie, loved to chase them down and sometimes killed them. I was creeped out by them and had Molly, then 5 years old, wear a long rubber glove while I held the garbage bag. She'd pick them up by the tail and stick them in the bag. It wasn't until a few years later that I learned about possum "playing dead." Good God, I may have made Molly pick up live possums!

I have a doggie door. One night around one in the morning, I heard a ruckus coming from downstairs. My dogs were barking and running in circles through the living room, dining room and kitchen. I came down the stairs and saw a possum "playing dead" at the bottom of the stairs. I ran back into my room and closed the door. "What the fuck am I gonna do?" I took a wire hanger and untwisted it for a weapon. I came from my room, started down the stairs, and jumped over the railing a few feet up so I wouldn't have to walk past him. I called the police for help. By now the possum was up and walking, then hid behind the coat rack. I could see his beaty eyes peeking out while he hissed at me. When the cops arrived, one came into the house and we both stood there looking at the possum. He asked me if I had a broom. As I went to get the broom, the other cop came in, walked over to the possum, picked him up by the back of the neck, opened the front door and stuck him in my tree. The other cop and I just looked at each other like we were useless buffoons.

For Molly's 18th birthday, I allowed her to have a party in the house. I instructed all the kids not to let the cops in should they arrive. I just had a feeling. I stayed upstairs while about 30 kids partied downstairs. Sure enough, around 10pm, the cops arrived. The kids followed my instructions and even turned off all the lights and lied down on the floor. I got on my hands and knees and crawled to Conor's room. I peeked out the window and a cop immediately shone a flashlight in my face. I quickly lied down. I yelled downstairs "Nobody move! Stay quiet!" We waited about 30 minutes until all 4 cop cars left. But then we saw that one of them was still lingering. I came downstairs and told the kids we had to wait a while, then they could start leaving in small groups. I couldn't find Molly. I looked all over for her. Apparently, she had climbed out the 2nd floor window, shimmied along the deck canopy frame and crawled over the 6-foot fence. She watched everything unfold from a block away. The only kid who didn't listen to me was my own.

I'm in blue, Molly's in grey.

Molly B ❤️

> Got my UD goin on

Today 10:37 AM

MOM

TAKE THAT HAT OFF

> Why? It's school spirit! This hat cost me $120,000!

I have a friend who grew up in Brooklyn, NY. As an adult, she moved to Point Pleasant. Unlike those of us who grew up here, she was hyper aware of her surroundings and much more distrustful than the rest of us. One day she was driving her kids to school and noticed a van driving very slowly on pace with two middle school-aged girls who were walking on the sidewalk. My friend was very suspicious of the driver of the van and felt compelled to park her car and run down the sidewalk towards the girls. As she got closer, she yelled "Do NOT get into that van!" The girls were startled and explained that the driver was their dad. He didn't want them walking to school alone.

While Molly was in college, I'd often send her stupid ass texts. I'm in grey, Molly's in blue.

•oooo AT&T 🔉   5:58 PM   @ 83% 🔋⚡

< Messages (1) **Mom**   Details

I put $50 on ur flex

> I saw thanks

I love you

> I love you too

You're pretty

> who is this..

You have nice feet

> who the fuck is this

Read 5:56 PM

It's me. Don't know what came over me. Can't stop laughing.

iMessage

My then-boyfriend's nephew played football for Yale University. He asked me to come with him to a game at Yankee Stadium in late October. We drove up early and started the day at a bar across the street from the stadium where the players' families and friends would gather to pre-game. It was about 1:00 and the bar was packed. A lot of his family were there, most of whom I'd not yet met. I waited for him to start the introductions, but I saw that he was up at the bar doing shots. Already I thought "Good God, how the hell am I gonna get home?" We stayed at the bar for a couple of hours and headed across to the stadium. We sat with his brother-in-law and a couple of friends. It was FREEZING. I had dressed warmly but my feet were ice cubes. He had continued drinking during the game, which was not like him. At half time I told him I was going to the gift shop in hopes that it might be heated. No luck. With Yankee Stadium being used primarily during baseball season, there was no heat anywhere in the stadium. When I returned to my seat, he was not there. I watched most of the rest of the game by myself, shivering. Near the end of the game, I went a few rows back and found his brother. I explained that I hadn't seen him since half time. He and I circled the entire stadium looking for him in all the bars. When we returned, there he was sitting in his seat. I was furious and didn't even want to talk to him. Apparently, he was quite inebriated. I asked his brother to tell him I wanted to go home, but not with him. The brother got the car keys from him and promised he'd take him home. So, I drove his car back to Point Pleasant Beach. Ugh. What a day.

I am not a day drinker, much to many of my friends' chagrin. I've always, in a very annoying, motherly-hen way, cautioned them that "it's a slippery slope, my friends." There have been a couple of times when I've made an exception to that rule. Once I was at my niece's baby shower. It started around noon as many showers do. Normally I would drink water. On this day I don't know what came over me, but I decided to drink vodka. I'm not even a vodka drinker. I've always been a wine or beer drinker. The shower was at B2 Restaurant in Point Pleasant Beach in the lovely, upstairs room. As part of the festivities, we were all given a tiny baby diaper and asked to write something on it. Anything. Something that would remind them of you, something cute, something funny. So, in bold letters I wrote across the diaper the word "CONDOMS."

I needed some rooms in my house painted. A high school friend had a local painting business, so I hired her for the job. There were four rooms that needed painting. One was a large, third floor family room with twenty-foot ceilings. She got started on that room in January. Turns out she was afraid of heights, so I helped her by climbing up the ladder behind her and putting my hand on her ass when she reached the top. It took several weeks to finish that room. One day I came home and saw her wearing a Charlie Brown tee shirt with Lucy's face on the front. I said "Wow, I have that tee shirt, too!" In a burst of laughter, she said "Yes, it's yours!"

My sister and I took my kids to Hershey Park when they were 11 and 8. We stayed at the Hershey Hotel, a majestic, historic 4-star hotel. As we waited in the lobby for our room to be ready, I pulled out something I thought would make the trip even more fun. A fart machine. For those of you who've not experienced the hilarity a fart machine can bring, I'll explain. There are two parts. One is a small plastic speaker where the fart sound emanates. The other is a remote control that allows you to choose from 4 different fart sounds which are the long, steady release, the short burst of a fart, the stutter fart, and the tiny blip of a fart. No matter how mature and sophisticated you may think you are, you cannot help but laugh when you hear the fart and see people's reactions. So, there we sat in this luxurious lobby with spectacular chandeliers, magnificent 20th century furniture, and 2-story wood paneled walls and ceilings. I showed the fart machine to my sister and the kids and got ready to try it out for the first time. We placed the speaker in a couch cushion about 20 feet away from us and waited for someone to sit down. An elderly woman and her husband sat down a few minutes later. Conor hit the remote control while we all waited to see the reaction. As soon as he hit it, the woman punched her husband in the arm and mumbled what we were sure were words of disgust.

In the amusement park there were so many opportunities to use the fart machine. Just walking along and hitting the remote could cause people to jump in surprise, glare at us in revulsion, and/or start giggling.

The hotel pool was also a good spot for the fart machine. Molly wrapped the fart machine in a towel and placed it under an empty lounge chair across the pool. There was man lying in the lounge chair next to it. We waited for someone to lie on the empty chair. Finally, a beautiful young woman with a big, wide rimmed sun hat, a bikini and high heels put down her towel on the lounge chair. As soon as she got all settled, Molly hit the remote control. Not just once, but 3 times in a row. The man immediately rolled to his side, away from the woman and began hysterically laughing. We could see the woman was trying to convince the man that it wasn't her. We were all in tears from the laughter.

In my younger years I had no idea that I suffered from severe anxiety. It wasn't something people talked about back then. The first time I suffered the symptoms, I was working as Assistant Marketing Director at the Woodbridge Mall. One of my first responsibilities was to speak before 250 mall merchants. I was so nervous. Sweaty hands, pounding heart. Just as I was about to walk on stage, my manager said "Don't worry, you'll do great. Just don't say 'Good Eileen, my name is Evening'." Rattled, I walked on stage and nearly vibrated right off the stage.

Despite my anxiety, I always seemed to put myself in the position of having to speak publicly. I was president of our local Board of Education for many years. One of my duties was to make the speeches at Elementary commencements and High School graduations. Knowing that if I could make the audience laugh, it would be much easier for me. That's a risky approach, cause if they don't laugh, I'm in trouble. At Conor's graduation, I approached the podium and the first thing I said was "My greatest fear in life is public speaking. And in closing."

I served on the Finance Committee at my local church, St. Peter's. We were having a capital campaign and the Pastor asked me to speak at Mass to encourage participation. I began by telling a story about how when we were kids, my Mom would take us to church. Then when all three of us were old enough to ride bikes at 12, 10 and 8, my Dad would give us 50 cents each for the collection basket. And off we'd go….to Hoffman's Donuts. We'd then swing by church and send my brother in for the bulletin for evidence we'd been there.

As a kid and young adult, I always struggled in the greeting card aisle. Father's Day was the hardest. I'd search through the cards looking for the right one but would never find it. "Thank you, Dad, for taking me fishing, on trips, and for always showing me how much you love me." Nope. Not that one. "Dad, you're the best! There's no Dad better than you!" No, that won't work. I sometimes imagined starting my own greeting card company. I'd name it "Mediocre Greeting Cards." It would be for moms, dads, friends, family who weren't quite as good as they could be. "Dad, you're not bad!" "Dad, you're usually there for me," "Dad, you always remember my name!"

While my dad was an engineer by trade, his love was always literature, poetry, and music. He would sometimes write short stories. Here's one called "A Quart of Milk."

Let me tell you a story about a quart of milk. I suppose that piqued your interest since no one ever tells a story about a quart of milk. Many days in the past, Winnie and I married. She was then and is now a fine person, my friend and confidant. A quart of milk was enough for our tea and coffee. And in short order, the Almighty blessed us with a "Babby." So, we went on for three quarts of milk. Two more "Babbies" raised the consumption to the gallons. Merci for our ability to provide. So, the years marched on, and oceans of milk were consumed. Children have a way of growing up. Ours were no exception. In a twinkling, the number of gallons required daily diminished. Well, the birds have flown the nest. Last week we bought a quart of milk. It will be enough.

My kids and I went to Ireland with my sister's family and our cousins. There were 10 of us. We travelled all over the

Emerald Isle on a tour bus. It was one of the greatest trips ever. My sister and I wanted to bring our Dad's ashes to Ireland and spread them there. Neither of us wanted our suitcases to be overweight, so we decided to split the ashes in half. I started to pour his ashes from the urn into a Ziplock bag. It didn't go well. His ashes were floating everywhere. In my hair, on my clothes. I'm not sure how much of him never made it into either bag. In Ireland we decided to spread some of his ashes at the Cliffs of Moher. They are stunning cliffs hundreds of feet high with beautiful, green grass and breathtaking ocean views. It was perfect. So, we spread half the ashes there and needed to pick a second place. Our bus driver, who would drink with us every night before driving us back to our hotel, said we needed to go to St. Brigid's Well. "Me Da's ashes are there. Aw, sure, that's the place for your Da!" So off we went to St. Brigid's Well. It was a shrine of sorts, cut into a mountain side. People would leave trinkets to remember the dead. Little Virgin Mary statues, rosary beads, mementos. In front of the cave was the well. All of us stood around the well so we could pass Dad's ashes to each other and give a little sprinkle. As soon as we gathered around the well, we realized it wasn't quite what we expected. It looked more like a sewer, with metal bars covering the well which held stagnant water. We started to pass the ashes and, one by one, started giggling. We were trying to hold it together as it was to be an important, heartfelt moment. Our shoulders were jiggling up and down. Bystanders wanted to get in on the fun. They didn't know what was going on but joined us in the spreading of the ashes into the sewer.

Following the Ireland leg of the trip, my kids and I went onto Paris for four days. After so much together time, we all had had enough of each other, but we were making the best of it. I fell in love with the escargot and kept trying to get the kids to taste it. On our last night, I convinced them.

We were in a lovely Parisian café. I ordered a big platter of escargot, in the shells. Conor grabbed the tongs that hold the shell while you pull out the snail. He grabbed the snail a little too hard and it shot across the table and hit Molly right smack in the forehead. Without a second of hesitation, as the hot pesto sauce ran down her nose, she stood up and "pow!" punched Conor. The French waiters were appalled. After I explained that it was an accident and got them settled down, I noticed the snail in its shell spinning around under our table, on the floor. "Hmmm" I thought. "It's probably still good." So, I reached down and grabbed it. Ugly Americans.

From 1990 to 2002, I worked at Goldman Sachs in Princeton, NJ. The plan was announced to move our offices to Jersey City. I was living in Point Pleasant Beach and thought the hour and 15-minute commute to Princeton was long enough. Going to Jersey City would make it even longer. I had just gotten divorced, and my kids were only 4 and 7, so I decided to think about other options. I started searching for a business I could start that would enable me to work from home. I found a methodology called "Cost Containment." I could buy a license and pay royalties to the founder. The methodology enabled the licensee to seek out clients of 50 employees or more, negotiate lower pricing with their incumbent suppliers, and share the savings with the client. I had absolutely no experience in this world, but I thought it sounded interesting. My friend at Goldman lived in Bucks County, PA. He also didn't like the idea of commuting to Jersey City. I was a little leery of trying on my own, so I asked him if he wanted to start the company with me. He agreed. We took the next few months, while still at Goldman, to form the LLC and prepare to launch the company. All the while we were trying to convince our bosses to lay us off so we could get a severance but had no luck.

The first couple of years were difficult. We made very little money but knew it would be worth sticking with it. Eventually we began signing clients. They were primarily in NJ, PA, and NY, but some were out of the area. We would travel to California, Florida, Georgia or wherever the client was. As a "cost containment" company, we lived by our name. We stayed in the cheapest hotels we could find. A few of them were doozies. We once stayed at a Howard Johnson's. It included breakfast. We met in the lobby and found a loaf of white bread and a jar of jelly there for us.

My business partner and I both like our wine. After spending the days at client sites, we'd come back to our hotel which never was fancy enough to have a bar. So we'd go on the hunt, on foot to find the nearest liquor store. Most times there was no liquor store nearby, but the 7-

Elevens sold little single serve bottles of wine. So, we'd find ourselves crossing 4 lane roadways in our business suits and crawling over concrete medians in search of our wine.

My little brother, Stephen, was a character. So funny, and always getting in trouble. I was going though old photo albums and found his school pictures from 3rd, 4th, and 5th grades. He had the same shirt on in all 3 pictures as well as a big fever sore on his lip, or as we Irish call it, "The Irish Crud." I don't know if it's truly something the Irish are predisposed to, but our whole family, including my dozens of first cousins all suffered with them.

The grips of alcohol and drugs got a hold of Stephen. In his twenties he struggled terribly, in and out of rehab and trying desperately to stay sober. In his late twenties he finally was able to stay sober for an entire year. Things were looking up for him. He was an apprentice union electrician working at the Claridge Hotel in Atlantic City. Then, on New Year's Eve and became very sick and was admitted to the hospital. After some tests, they determined that he was HIV positive; he had contracted it through needle sharing. It was devastating news for all of us. This was in 1991 when there was supposedly no hope for someone with HIV. It was assumed that it would ultimately become AIDS. Of course, we know better now, but for Stephen it was a death sentence. One night at 2am I got a phone call from him. He was crying. "I'm so scared" he sobbed. My heart was breaking for him. "I know I'm gonna die" he said. I tried to comfort him and tell him there's always hope, but not seeing any future for himself, he later overdosed on methadone at 30 years of age.

Stephen had a lot of talent. He was an awesome singer and often performed with his best friend, his cousin, Tommy. He was funny, sneaky, warm, caring, and adorable. We all miss him terribly.

My sweet, loving Mom died at age 55. Her esophagus burst and they were unable to control the bleeding. It was all so sudden. We were heartbroken. The day after her funeral, I was driving back to my apartment in Jersey City. It was Christmas week and very cold. As I exited the turnpike, a warm breeze blew through my car. The windows were closed. It was strong enough to blow my hair. It was the smell of my mom, her perfume. Not long after that, every night as I was falling off to sleep, I could sense someone sitting at the foot of my bed. Then the covers were pulled up over my shoulder as if I were being tucked in. I wouldn't open my eyes. I was scared. I knew it was my Mom. After six nights of this, I got the courage to say out loud "I love you, Mom, but you're scaring the shit out of me!" She never came back.

After my Dad sold our childhood home "as is," my sister and I couldn't bring ourselves to meet the new owners. We knew what they inherited. By selling the house "as is" and leaving with nothing but a ditty bag, our Dad didn't have to worry about packing up and cleaning out. He didn't have to clear out the guest room dresser drawers with clothing and hypodermic needles left behind. He didn't have to bother disposing of the dozens of large black leaf bags filled with empty Budweiser cans in the garage. Nor did he have to collect all the family photo albums. He could leave everything behind. So, a few years passed, and the new family totally renovated the house. We were dying to see what they'd done but were embarrassed to introduce ourselves. Then a day came when I had to visit the house for some PTO pickup. I introduced myself, but the owner said "Yes, I know who you are. When we moved in, your childhood pictures were on the walls." I said "Oh, yes. I'm so sorry for how my Dad left the house." She was so sweet and understanding that I thought it would be okay to ask for a tour. They had done a beautiful job. She took me through the whole house and at the end she showed me the backyard. They had built a gorgeous pool area with waterfalls and beautiful landscaping. As I stood looking, I turned to her husband and said "sorry." He just smiled and nodded his head. He knew why I was apologizing. A few years before my Dad sold the house, he no longer wanted the upkeep of our inground pool. So, he had it bulldozed in. Everything. The sliding board, diving board, ladders, pool deck and pool furniture. And covered it with 3 inches of topsoil.

My Dad was a creature of habit. He loved to go to the local bar, Frankie's, in Point Pleasant Beach. He'd go every day in the afternoon and have two beers. He was a real fixture there. Even had his own barstool. After he passed, we noticed that a lot of the staff at Frankie's came to his funeral. It was unexpected and very sweet. At his repass, I stood and thanked everyone for coming and gave a eulogy for my Dad. I said "My sister and I figured out why the

Frankie's staff were all broke up about his passing. When we went through his paperwork, we saw credit card bills which had daily charges from Frankie's. He would have two $3 beers and leave a $20 tip. So, when we did the calculation, that was $91,000 in total over the years." They lost a great tipper.

When Molly was 4 years old, she and I were in Walmart. We were at the jewelry counter. Suddenly, loud enough for everyone around us to hear, she asked "Mommy, why does that lady have a moustache?"

I was job hunting in the mid-90's and needed to update my resume. I had a friend who was a professional editor and she helped me revise it. Just for fun, we created two resumes – one serious and one silly. Well, I mistakenly sent out the silly one to several prospective employers. It described my life dream as being able to go to Africa and chase wild elephants. It explained in one job description that "I didn't really know what I was doing. It was very confusing." In another that "My boss was a lazy ass and made me do all the work." And in yet another job description "I was really just in it for the money. I didn't give a hoot if my team made their numbers." I listed my personal activities as "Frequent Happy Hour Attendee," "Member of the Fiddle De Fizz Irish Step Dancing Team," "Boogie Boarding for Old Broads Team Captain," and "Online Dating Specialist."

My sister and I went on a pub crawl in Ireland. It was a bus tour through the west of Ireland with a tour guide who stood at the front of the bus holding a microphone, giving us the history of the surrounding area, pointing out some of the spectacular landscapes, and throwing in some Irish humor for the laughs. Our Dad was somewhat of an expert on all subjects Irish. He was an American but seemed to know more about Irish history and geography than most people born and raised in Ireland. As kids we would often listen to him tell stories of the Irish rebels, Sinn Fein, the atrocities committed by the English upon the Irish, and such. Well as we drove along the beautiful hills of County Mayo, we heard the tour guide tell a story about how the Irish potato famine had killed a million Irish people, and why it happened. We'd heard that story many times from our Dad, but the tour guide was telling a contrary version of it. My sister and I looked at each other and exclaimed "Dad was wrong!" We were a little happy about that because he was never wrong. And as the tour guide finished telling the story, he said "Well that's how most people think it happened, but here's the real story!" Of course, the real story was Dad's story.

When my kids were seven and four years old, I got us a Wave Runner for Christmas. When summer came, I took them out on the Manasquan River for our first tour. It was a 3-seater, so it was perfect. We had so much fun zipping around, jumping wakes and exploring Treasure Island. I decided it would be fun to go out through the Inlet to the ocean. It's hard to tell how rough the seas are until you're fairly close to the mouth of the inlet. There were lots of boats coming in and out, so I couldn't see whether it was safe for us to go. As we approached the mouth, I could see that the swells were pretty big, but I knew I couldn't be wishy-washy about it. I had to either gun it or turn around. I decided to go. As we're jumping the swells toward the ocean, my son Conor was behind me yelling "No, Mommy, no!" My daughter, Molly, in front of me raised her fist and yelled "Go, Mommy, go!"

Molly and I went to the water park in Seaside Heights when she was 10 years old. We both loved water parks, so we'd get our own tube and ride for hours. On one slide, I lost my tube halfway down and had to scoot on my ass the rest of the way. I dropped into the pool at the end of the slide. While climbing out, the elderly man working the slide said "Miss, um, your bathing suit is shredded." I quickly sat down and scanned the park for Molly. I finally saw her and called her over to help me. I took her by the hands and drew her face to my ass so we could walk back to our seats.

As a project manager at Goldman Sachs in the IT department, I was part of a team that visited a software developer for a demo on a new General Ledger system. Halfway through the 3-hour demo, I needed a cigarette. I excused myself saying I had to use the ladies' room. I saw there was a balcony off the lunch area. I opened the glass sliding doors and lit up. Within one minute the skies opened and, with no roof on the balcony, it started to downpour. I tried to get back in, but the sliding glass door was locked. I was already drenched. I finally got the attention of an employee and got in. I then went to the ladies' room. I was a disaster. I was completely drenched, mascara running down my face. I stuck my head under the hand dryer, but it didn't help much. I managed to clean up the mascara but couldn't do anything about my hair and clothes. I walked back into the demo as if nothing happened.

When the kids were old enough to ride their bikes to the elementary school, I would often run out onto the front porch to wave goodbye. I loved embarrassing them. As they pulled out of the driveway on their bikes, with other kids riding by as well, I'd yell loudly, "Have a great day! Mommy loves you! Eat all your lunch! Don't pick your nose!"

EPILOGUE

I truly hope you had some laughs at my expense. Nothing would make me happier.

I'd like to thank my Aunt Chris for inspiring me to write the damn book. If you'd like to read more about my Mom's life in Ireland and her journey to America, you can read "Go, Lassie, Go!" by Christine Mulvaney.

I am blessed with the best friends in the world. They have helped me through rough times and helped create some of the best times. When I'm with you all, there's endless laughter. I love you all. You know who you are!

To my Flarity and Brennan families, we've all been through so much together and apart, and have come out on the other side stronger for it. Cousins are the best!

And for my Conor and Molly, please know I did my best. I'm so proud of you both. Remember, always, the words I hope have inspired you, "FORGIVENESS, ACCEPTANCE, GRATITUDE, LOVE."

Made in the USA
Coppell, TX
28 September 2023